LADY BITS AND PIECES

A funny, poetic look at life,
love and lady stuff

ROSEMARY GREGORY

FINE: Fucked up Insecure Neurotic
Emotional

To sisters, everywhere.

LADY BITS AND PIECES

Rosemary Gregory
rosemaryg@hotmail.co.uk
www.rosemarygregory.co.uk

Cover design and typesetting by greyz
www.greyzdesign.com

Published by R&R Publishing

ISBN: 978-0-9571125-1-3

A day without
laughter is a
day wasted

Charlie Chaplin

LADY BITS AND PIECES

About the author:

Rosemary lives in Warwickshire.
She retired from teaching two years ago and
started writing and performing poetry.
She also does stand up comedy and acts as an
MC when asked; or even when not.
This is Rosemary's second book. Her first book,
Grey Matters, deals with the subject of getting
older, and includes poetry about bus-passes,
shampoo and mobile phones.

A message from the author:

This book has a slightly different format from my first book of poems.
There is a theme for the first part of the book, Lady Bits which is about shared experiences some women may have, and in no way applies to any particular woman or all women.
Any resemblance to anyone living or otherwise is purely coincidental. Some poems may be autobiographical; most are not.

The second section is what it says on the cover; Bits and Pieces. I feel that some of these random poems need an explanation of how they came about, so have included this where deemed useful.

As with my first book, this whole selection of poems is, in my view, better when read aloud.
As before, I've included a selection of quotes and one-liners that make me smile.

The first section is not in any particular order to reflect life's sequence. Some of the poems are happy and funny and one or two are sad, which is exactly as it should be.

LADY BITS

BITS AND PIECES

If you can't be a good example, then you'll just have to be a horrible warning

Catherine Aird

Love Rant benefitted from a wonderful website I found called 'Valentine Pet Name Generator'; very useful for all those times when you just can't think of what you want to call your loved one.
Well worth a visit!

LOVE RANT

I HATE LOVE
The ribbons and chocolates and flowers
You gaze at each other, and sigh quite a lot
And you talk on the phone for two hours

I HATE LOVE
All that planning your future together
The cottage with roses, the cats and the kids
And a mortgage that ties you forever

I HATE LOVE
There's your special place down by The Lanes
And 'Our Song' which you know was just written for you
And you choose quite ridiculous names

I HATE LOVE
Names like Fluffy or Sparkly-Love-Comet
Or Butter-Babe-Sweetums or Monkey-Cheeks-Lambkin
Rose-Sunshine-Doll just makes me vomit

I HATE LOVE
All those poems and songs about hearts
Whereas most of the focus it just seems to me
Is on lower down bodily parts

I HATE LOVE
All those hormones make people quite odd
You're in heaven just holding the hand of a man
You mistakenly think is a god

I HATE LOVE
Smooching pairs simply make me feel stroppy
All that moonlight and sighing and swooning
and stars
But it's messy and sticky and sloppy

I HATE LOVE
The films and the stories and verse
End in happily after, but don't tell you how
I just can't think of anything worse

I HATE LOVE
When the hours pass by in a minute
But mainly the reason I hate bloody love
Is because I am no longer in it

Love is a temporary insanity, easily cured by marriage
Ambrose Bierse

The next poem, Above Rubies, contains a puzzle.
From the various clues, can you work out the year
when Ben and Lucy were born? (they were born in
the same year)
There isn't a prize, by the way…..

Above Rubies

Ben and Lucy met at school when they were
only ten
She was a living doll, he pulled her hair to show
he cared
She wiggled in her hula hoop and shyly gave a smile
He rode his rocket bicycle as quickly as he dared

He kissed her by the new bike-sheds when they
were just fourteen
Each other's gift for Christmas was 'I want to hold
your hand'
As Beatles sang, they kissed again beneath
the mistletoe
Ben knew that Lucy was the one, he knew
she'd understand

At sweet sixteen they were a couple,
starry eyes aglow
'I got you babe' was their own song, so sure of
what they'd got
In 'Carry on Cowboy' at the Ritz, Ben whispered 'I
love you'
She whispered back 'I love you too, I love you such
a lot'

Engaged at twenty one, they had a ring on
every finger
They planned their life, some hens, a cat, some
sons and lots of daughters
In massive flares and beads and bells they danced
the whole night long
He sang to her he'd be her bridge over the
troubled waters,

As Europe joined in union, Lucy and Ben united
Lucy wore a cheesecloth robe; Ben wore a
kaftan too
'Walking on the wild side' was the wedding song
they'd chosen
Their hair was long and flowing, with wild flowers
threaded through

Now many years since they first wed, their
sons and daughters grown
They've laughed and cried, and fought and
loved through fair and stormy weather
And now with wine and candlelight reflect-
ing in their eyes
Ben and Lucy celebrate the years they've
spent together

Coldplay's 'Paradise' is playing, there's a
sudden flash
A tiny fairy, scarlet winged, flies from the
candle flame
Her crimson hair and carmine dress reflect
a rosy glow
She waves her sparkling garnet wand, says
'Ruby is my name'

'For all these years you've both been true, I
grant you each a wish
What you desire can now be yours; this
wish is automatic
Though once you say your wish out loud it
cannot be undone'
She crackles in the candlelight; she is a
touch dramatic

Ben and Lucy look amazed, the fairy twirls and smiles
Lucy thinks for a short time, says 'I know what I'll choose'
She takes Ben's hand and smiles a gentle smile into his eyes
'I'd like to take my husband on a luxury world cruise'

The garnet wand just flashes twice, and Lucy has two tickets
Now Ben replies, 'I'd love a cruise, to Spain or the far-east,
Dear Lucy, please I hope that you'll forgive, and understand
I'd like to go with someone younger, thirty years at least.'

The fairy smiles a small sad smile and shakes her head in sorrow
Twirls in the air and waves her wand which sparkles prettily
'Thirty years younger is your wish, I grant it to you sadly'
A double flash, vermillion smoke and Ben is ninety three

I'm not offended by all the dumb blonde jokes because I know I'm not dumb, and I'm also not blonde.

Dolly Parton

Whatever!

I've fallen in love from a distance before
And worshipped a man I don't know
Then finally meet him and usually find
My passion will quite quickly go

Some men I forget till I see them again
Then I love them whenever we meet
But as soon as they leave and are out of my sight
I forget that I thought they were sweet

But wherever you are I will love you, my love
You can be just where you want to be
You can stay if you wish, or can go far away
It just doesn't matter to me

Sex with love is the greatest thing in
life. But sex without love - that's
not so sad either

Mae West

Have you ever noticed how, in Soulmate advertisements, some men seem to have slightly unrealistic expectations?

Desperately Seeking

Own house and car, G.S.O.H.,
Likes theatre and art
This handsome and successful man
Seeks woman who is smart

Likes country walks and evenings in
Goes daily to the gym
This suave, sophisticated man
Seeks woman who is slim

Likes intellectual discourse
Reads Rousseau and Voltaire
This dashing, classy, modish man
Seeks girl with long, blonde hair

Likes concerts and the opera
Well-groomed and so well dressed
This man with fashion sense and style
Seeks lady with large chest

Romantic and quite passionate
Knows how to be discreet
This witty, warm and tactile male
Seeks female who's petite

Likes dining out with vintage wine
With talk that is refined
This energetic male with class
Seeks female with broad mind

If you're petite and willowy
Just call and make a date
This bachelor of sixty-six
Seeks girl of twenty eight

Hmmm… (a bit of a reply)

This woman who is twenty eight
Finds it an aberration
That all men think that they'll attract
A younger generation

So just get real and change your ways
Think carefully old man
And choose a woman your own age
The same age as my gran!

A male gynaecologist is like an auto mechanic who never owned a car.

Carrie Snow

One plus one doesn't always make two

When I was one alone
I danced to my own tune
I made up my own songs to sing
and sang them as I flew
I loved the simple music that I made
when I was one alone

Then you found me
I had not realised I was lost
Now I was half of two
We sang and harmonised together
and danced as if we had one body
I loved the music that we made
when I was half of two

Now I am one alone again,
I have lost my music
I have forgotten how I danced and sang
I no longer have any songs
You took my tunes with you
when you left me to be one alone again
I am no longer half of two
No longer even one alone,
I now feel less than one

Gorgeous Grannies

The gorgeous granny belly dance all meet in the
school hall
Our children worry that we'll have a heart attack
or fall
They say we've no decorum
Us gorgeous grans ignore 'em
As we shimmer and we glimmer and we just don't
care at all

The cellulite and extra skin, it really doesn't matter
To do a proper belly dance, it's better if
you're fatter
We always feel delighted
When the audience get excited
We shimmy and we shake so all our sequins shine
and scatter

With tambourines and cymbals we can hide the
joints that creak
If people criticise us we just turn the other cheek
Our bodies undulate
In a sexy figure eight
We're gorgeous and we're beautiful for just an
hour each week

We wiggled and we sparkled as we
sensuously shook
To get us to perform for you just go
online and book
We 're making ourselves fitter
In our coin belts and our glitter
Google 'Gorgeous Grannies' if you want to take
a look

Forget all of your troubles and join us all next time
The costumes and the body moves are really
quite sublime
You only need a bus pass
To come and join our dance class
Come and belly dance with us while you're still in
your prime

A rule of thumb for all women: if it
has tyres or testicles, you're going to
have trouble with it.

Anon

Teenage Valentine's Day

There's a pink envelope on my doormat today
I'm afraid that it's not that exciting,
As I pick up my one, solo valentine card
I recognise my mother's writing

I try to take one day at a time,
but sometimes several days attack
me at once.

Jennifer Unlimited

Conversations through life

At seven we talk about whose mum is best
And why baby brothers are always a pest
We're swapping our stickers,
And showing our knickers
At seven we never feel stressed

And later we argue whose doll is the fairy
And why Frankie Griffin is so big and hairy
And how to learn spelling
And whose feet are smelling
At ten things can starts to get scary

At thirteen the talk is of music and songs
If Paul or if George is more sexy than John
So now we are flirts
In our very short skirts
The ducklings are changing to swans

Then makeup and clothes are the talk of
the day
And if Janet Morgan has gone all of the way
I'm snogging the yobs
Getting Saturday jobs
At sixteen my life is still play

As students it's Nietzche and feelings of doom
Political causes, world crises and gloom,
At just twenty one
I've no time to have fun
I'm saving the world from my room

At thirty the wedding is over and done
I'm pregnant - a sister for Noah, our son
House prices are soaring
At dinner it's boring
We talk about mortgages and the school run

At forty I'm single; our marriage is ended
He's left with a colleague, whom I once
befriended
Divorce is a nightmare
I find the first white hair
My teenage son just got suspended

At fifty my children have grown and are fine
Grandchildren continue the family line
Plants need attention
Our talk is of pensions
while drinking our home made plum wine

At 60 we talk about our misspent youth
The grey hairs and wrinkles revealing the truth
A toyboy or two
Can make us feel new
We'll show we're not long in the tooth

At 70 the talk is of family and savings
We're no longer bothered by passionate cravings
More calm and serene
We reflect on what's been
We're no longer drowning, just waving

When 80 it's hearing aids and embrocation
And who's had a burial and who a cremation
With lessened mobility
And greater fragility
We talk about our medication

At 90 we talk about whose mum was best
And why baby brothers were always a pest
We no longer worry
We're not in a hurry
At 90 we needn't feel stressed

New School

It's five years since my first contraction,
five years since my boy was born
First day at his primary school,
I'm feeling quite forlorn

Will he listen to the teacher,
take in all the stuff he hears?
Or like his dad be really naughty?
Dad's been that for thirty years

Will he eat the lunch I made him?
Will he make a new best friend?
Or will he hate and loathe the classroom
waiting for the day to end

Then there's bullies, tests and homework,
getting lost finding the loo
PE kit and tying laces,
there's so much he has to do

And remembering all his colours
and the letters in his name
I just don't think that I can cope,
tomorrow it all starts again

My second favourite household chore
is ironing. My first is hitting my
head on the top bunk bed until I
faint.

Erma Bombeck

Since you left

The dog doesn't eat or wag his tail any more
He stands by the door waiting for you to
come home

The oven seems to be broken
Meals taste like cardboard all the time

The clocks have all slowed down
Each minute is an hour long

The flowers in the garden are different species
They're all less brightly coloured and have lost
their scent

I need a new sofa, because where we snuggled up
Has stopped feeling cosy and comfortable

The photograph of you on the shelf
Now looks older and much sadder

The television shows we used to laugh at together
Don't seem to be on any more

Even the memory foam mattress remembers you
I fit myself into the shape where you used to lie

Ladies' night

The tickets sold out really fast
We bought ours in advance
Now Mr Bicep's on the stage
Making his torso dance

For ladies' nights the men stay home
While women hit the town
They go to watch young naked hunks
Gyrate their bodies round

These oiled and sinewed muscle men
Pose, thrust and strut with ease
But when they speak it seems quite clear
They've brains the size of peas

It isn't big or clever when
These hunks take off their clothes
And though we shriek and laugh and point
We don't want one of those

Find me a man who makes me laugh
And then I'll be impressed
And if he cooks and irons as well
He needn't get undressed

Happy Event

Though giving birth's a natural situation,
yoga class and keeping fingers crossed will
not prevent you having the sensation
of trying to force a grapefruit through
one nostril

Sometimes you kiss a lot of
frogs, and still finish up with
a toad.

Anon

This next poem was started while visiting Marks and Spencer's underwear department with my sister, and being bewildered by the range of knickers available. I researched styles, colours, patterns and slogans (there really are pants with the slogans I've used!) to gain more understanding of the subject.

Psychology of Pants

With full-brief or midi or mini or shorts
Then hipsters, brazilian or thong
Bikini or boy-shorts, control or knee bloomers
No wonder buying pants takes so long

The G-string is cache-sexe when purchased
in France
This translates as 'hide genitalia'
It's considered quite racy here in the UK
But is standard beach-wear in Australia

Beige bloomers are best known as
non-scoring drawers
Tanga's are thought to be flirty
The cami's for when you would like to seem chic
While thongs are just plain down and dirty

But pants can't be visible, hide them from view
Wear strings, magic, no V P L
High leg or bandeau, and having decided
You must choose the fabric as well

There's nylon or lace, cotton, silk or
there's chiffon
Wool thermal for in the cold weather
Satin or silky, or if you feel wicked
There's PVC, rubber or leather

Now coloured or pattered, the plain seems
quite simple
But coloured pants all have a meaning
Black or red are quite saucy, plain white
is for pure
While green shows a natural leaning

Purple's for mystery, yellow is happy
Orange says living life faster
Brown shows convention, or feeling unwell,
While grey was a washing disaster

Blue's for the peaceful and tranquil of mind
Pink is for youth without care
But your character shows even more
when you look
At the patterns on pants that you wear

Spotty is cheeky, while zag-zags are arty
Leopard print says really naughty
The floral is seasonal, snakeskin is weird
And stripes are considered quite sporty

Slogans are always a thing to avoid
Imagine you're sharing a bath
Your lover strips off showing pants that confess
That 'Sometimes I wee when I laugh'

'No-one understands me' announced via pants
Is not someone I'd choose to meet
Though maybe more worrying, you can get pants
Which promise a 'trick or a treat?'

The worst I encountered on underwear quotes
Would have anyone leaving quite fast
Imagine revealing a slogan that says
'I like you so I'll kill you last'

So choosing your pants is a minefield it seems
You can often be misunderstood
To avoid all the pitfalls and make no mistakes
I'm going commando for good

Visiting Mum

Oh hello, come on in,
Did you say you were coming today?
My memory's not quite what it was
Have I mentioned that before?

What day is it by the way?
Ah, yes. Course it is
I knew that all along
Would you like a cup of tea
I was only saying to thingummybob
You know, the chap next door

Just sit down and take the weight off your feet
Shall I make us a nice cup of tea?

You know
He used to work for whatshisname
Who made those things for cars
Or was it stuff for something else?
Doesn't really matter

My memory's not quite what it was
Have I mentioned that before?

Anyway, I was talking to him on Tuesday
Or was it Friday when we went to see… oh… you
know
It might have been Thursday
The day when the bin men come

Did you say you would like a cup of tea?

And I had a visit from that woman
You know whose father runs the pub
The one with the yellow cardigan

She asked me if I wanted to go somewhere
on Thursday
Or was it Tuesday
Now, was it bingo or flower arranging?
I'm sure it was something like that

My memory's not quite what it was
Have I mentioned that before?

Shall I put the kettle on?

She has that little cat
Or is it a dog?
Anyway,

She took me to see that nice young doctor
Who looks like the chap on telly
That programme with her out of
Coronation Street,
You know the blonde one
Or was she in Emmerdale?

My memory's not quite what it was
Have I mentioned that before?

Anyway
I told him I've been having trouble remembering
things ....sometimes
I can't see what all the fuss is about
But he said I need to go and see someone and
they'll let me know
At least I think that's what he said
You know one of those consultants
or something

I expect they can sort it out

Now, would you like some tea?

A woman never forgets her age
- once she decides what it is.

Anon

The next poem is from a workshop where we had
to imagine being wooed by someone in a particular
profession, and how they might persuade.
Imagining a sweet maker meant not much persua-
sion would be needed.

Sweet talker

You tempt my tongue
with sugared words and chocolate enticements
I mistrust the sticky treats you offer
You show me dark treasures
with sweet marzipan hearts,
and soft fondant centres
hiding shocks of almond
You lure me with milkily enclosed liquid fruits of
pleasure
With caramel and candy you try to win me
Reluctantly I allow your soufflé kisses
to melt my wafer thin resistance
My lips respond guiltily
to your crystallised promises
I feel my raw heart soften and melt
as you glaze me with honeyed spice.
Warm treacle trickles inside my spine
Sugared cream caresses my skin
awakening taste buds in all my limbs
Caressed by your buttery fingers
all my senses now crave your cloying
syrupy
sweetness

White Lace and Promises

To take thee as my lawful spouse
My darling we've waited for this
To promise our hearts to each other for life
And seal the whole thing with a kiss

'To have and to hold', well that seems ok
'From this day forward', till when?
'For better or worse', not so sure about that
'In sickness and health', come again?

A paper-cut sends him to bed for a week
It's A and E just for a cold
Hypochondria's all that he hasn't caught yet
Do I want that to have and to hold?

For richer for poorer, I'm really not sure
The small print did not make that clear
The money he earns is not really enough
To keep me in style for a year

Plus this is a man who can not find his socks
The laundry bag just works by magic
He can't boil an egg without phoning his mum
To marry him would be quite tragic

'Forsaking all others' – I don't think I can
When Johnny Depp makes my spine tingle
To stay with one man for the rest of your life
Makes it seem much more fun to stay single

'Till death us do part', seems a little extreme
A better idea with less strain
'Till divorce us do part' then at least we can go
And get on with our lives while still sane

'For better for worse', that still doesn't sound right
Let's forget it and just be good friends
Do the cinema, dinner and walks in the park
And just live in sin at weekends

I never married, because there was no
need. I have three pets at home which
answer the same purpose as a hus-
band. I have a dog that growls every
morning, a parrot that swears all af-
ternoon, and a cat that comes home
late every night.

Marie Corelli

For those who haven't come across vajazzles (as I hadn't until recently), these are adhesive sparkles glued onto any of those ' intimate' places only to be seen by that select few (select few in most cases anyway) They last for a few days (the vajazzles, not the select few).

Give them the old razzle dazzle

I went to town to meet my chap
A married man called Basil
I had an hour or so to spare
So I got a fun vajazzle

In intimate and secret spots
You stick them on your flesh
There's shapes or names in sparkly gems
Bright jewels stuck on mesh.

I thought about what I should get
For only him to see
A crystalline vajazzle kit
To make a shiny 'B'

Now Basil's once more single
As his wife found it quite weird
That he came home from his work with 'B'
Vajazzled in his beard

Cougar

Never trust a cougar
A woman on a mission
Although you'll get some practise
In every known position

Beware the temptress cougar
With her entrancing spell
She'll take her selfish pleasure
And leave a dried out shell

Don't listen to a cougar
Who only has one goal
She'll suck out all your juices
And then devour you whole

And if you meet a cougar,
Maybe it sounds like fun
She'll use you for diversion
And leave you when she's done

Stay away from cougars
Those women full of lust
They'll chew you up and spit you out
A sorry pile of dust

So don't believe the cougar
You'll lose, I guarantee
To keep you safe from danger
You could come home with me!

The title for this poem comes from a rather cruel, unkind game we played as much younger and less considerate women. We would classify men according to how many glasses of alcohol we would need to drink to find them desirable.

Ten-glasser

The Gargoyle comes right over and asks me what
I'm drinking
His garlic breath would stop a loaded
Eddie Stobart truck
His belly stretches his striped shirt right to
its very limits
Tonight this man is so far out of luck

Back to the bar it's my turn now to get another
round in
I'm sticking to a whisky chaser with my large
red wine
I'm told I get a little frisky if I have too many
But at this minute I'm still feeling fine

The Gargoyle has a comb-over; it really isn't sexy
A Guinness and Ribena now seems like such a
good idea
My friend Anne's having vodka, so I'll get myself
a single
The Gargoyle gives me quite a sexy leer

The dandruff on his collar is reflecting in the
strip light
This brandy and pineapple tastes quite strong
He sent a little wink to me, I sent a quick
one back
Ignoring him is rude and feels just wrong

I've always liked maturer men, they have their
life more sorted
It doesn't mean I'll marry him if he buys me
a gin
A sherry with a snakebite and I stagger to
his corner
The lucky feller is about to win

Love handles seem quite sexy and I give him a
quick cuddle
And what's wrong with a shiny, shabby suit?
The halitosis is less strong now that I've a
double whisky
And comb-overs can really look quite cute

When a woman behaves like a man,
why doesn't she behave like a nice
man?
Anon

This originally started as a song with a blues style guitar accompaniment and was written many years ago, when I was fairly newly married with young children.

Boredom Blues

Hubby's gone off to catch the 8.15
It's my job to keep the happy homestead clean
My head is aching and my feet are itching
If something don't change, I'm gonna blow
up the kitchen

I've got the blues
Got the boring old boredom blues
Got the greasy dishwater, smelly underpants blues

Books and films all told me being a mother and wife
Was the ultimate fulfilment I could get out of life
If I don't like what I'm supposed to be
It's plain that there must be something
wrong with me

I've got the blues
Got the boring old boredom blues
Got the reading Woman's Own,
cooking sherry's gone blues

When I was a girl I thought that a kiss
Could open the door to everlasting bliss
You'd marry your love and be his only one
Tell me where have my dreams all gone?

I've got the blues
Got the boring old boredom blues
Got the kids all need new shoes, pass me the
vallium blues

Did you have a good day at the office my dear?
Your dinner's on the table and your slippers are here
The television's easier than conversation
As we seem to have a breakdown in communication

I've got the blues
Got the boring old boredom blues
Got the head is full of dust, vacuum cleaner's bust

Shopping, cooking, cleaning, washing,
comforting, mending
Seems a housewife's day is never ending
One day I'll leave, gonna set myself free
Maybe have a chance to find out about me

I've got the blues
Got the boring old boredom blues
Got the three foot ironing pile,
forgotten how to smile
Should have stayed in bed, might as well be dead
End without an end, drive you round the bend blues

You don't get anything clean without getting something else dirty.

Cecil Baxter

This next poem uses the Victorian tradition of saying it with flowers.
Hopeful young men sent love messages via flowers, which all had very specific meanings. Their intended would reply in similar vein. Most of the meanings here are accurate, though I have added one or two suggestions of my own.

Orally and Florally

I sent her scarlet roses saying, darling I love you
Sweet violets declared my love for ever and a day
Forget-me-nots to signify my heart is
strong and true
She sent me back a thistle – 'go away!'

A posy of white daisies said 'I'm dazzled by
your charms'
A red carnation said 'my love is strong'
My honeysuckle garland meant 'I'd like
you in my arms'
Her sprig of hemlock told me I was wrong

A bunch of golden marigolds said she had
hurt my pride
White lilac was to show my love is deep
My flowering almond sent the hope she'd have
me at her side
Her bunch of weeds response said 'you're a creep'

Pink carnations showed my love would last and
always grow
My orange blossom was a marriage ballad
She sent back poison ivy saying 'There's no chance,
still no'
With leaves of deadly nightshade, for a salad

I promised wedded bliss with a bouquet of
prickly holly
A dried rose said she felt she'd rather die
She then sent a geranium, stupidity and folly
And death-cap fungus for her last good-bye

I have never hated a man enough to
give his diamonds back.

Zsa Gabor

ME, ME, ME

'I need more space for me' he said
'It isn't you, it isn't you
'I need to be more free,' he said
I listened

'I need to sort my head 'he said
'It isn't you, it isn't you
I need to find my way' he said
I listened

'I need some time alone' he said
'It isn't you, it isn't you
I need to know myself' he said
I listened

I heard and knew it wasn't me
'Goodbye, I wish you well' I said
I left

Whatever women must do they must
do twice as well as men to be
thought half as good. Luckily,
this is not difficult.

Anon

Your Mother !

I'm glad you left four weeks ago
And went off with another
But one thing must have slipped your mind
You left me with your mother

She never liked me, I was wrong
Not good enough for you
Not good enough for her dear son
In spite of all I do

She's in the front room as we speak
Just watching daytime telly
Complaining that the cat's been in
And made the cushions smelly!

And does she even know you've gone
Run off with that young tart
And did you ever think it might
Crack up that stony heart

So please come back and get your mum
To leave her's a bit steep
She criticizes all I do
And never seems to sleep

Or did you really think I could
Forget she's here with me
With all the washing, cooking and
The endless cups of tea

I just can't have her living here
She never liked me really
I've told her she can come to you
Because you love her dearly

She's scowling like a gargoyle and
She looks a lot like you
Skulking in the sitting room
And judging all I do

Your floozy might not like it though
It spelled the end for us
She'll be with you by 5 o'clock
I'll put her on the bus

The trouble with her is that she
lacks the power of conversation but
not the power of speech.

George Bernard Shaw

Heart Map

The surest way to a man's heart I heard was with
your cooking
I snared him with my onion rings, my roasties and
my steak
With egg and chips I won his love, my puddings
made him giddy
I made him mine with bakewell tart and date and
walnut cake

With treacle sponge I snared his heart, with creamy
mash and sausage
Full English breakfast kept him home, I fed him well
each day
Glazed carrots served with venison both kept him
on the sofa
With apple pie I kept him close,
he didn't need to stray

With cheese and pickle sandwiches, she lured
him from my side
For takeout curry he became a man who
was possessed
She couldn't offer haute cuisine, no gourmet
meals or snacks
A girly simper won his love - plus her
enormous chest

And even dauphinoise potatoes couldn't keep
him home
Spurned roasted chicken dinner was what led
to my arrest
I served it with a side dish, an alternate heart
route-way
The other way to my man's heart was a
breadknife through the chest

If you are what you eat, then I'm
fast, cheap and easy.

Anon

I think we now know each other well enough for the next poem.

Seven Floors in the Lift
(An alternate title is from my favourite grafitti, Harwich for the Continent, Frinton for the Incontinent)

While visiting the waterworks with the local W.I.
I had a really unappealing thought
The human water system should be mostly safe and dry
But mine is not behaving as it ought

I can't walk past a public loo,
Can't travel far with ease
A running tap's a torture sound,
I mustn't cough or sneeze

'Down there' I whispered to the doc, 'There's something going wrong'
'Well, at your age,' the doctor said 'Your pelvic floor's not strong'

'Down there' I told the second doc 'I think I've sprung a leak!'
He nodded sagely and replied
'Your pelvic floor is weak'

The physio can see you right.
Best pants for Gina Gym
'Squeeze and relax, let's see how strong!'
My muscle power is grim

A healthy floor's about a 6,
I really had to laugh
My muscles measured in at just a
lousy less than half

Squeeze and relax just 10 more times.
Imagine it's a lift
With seven floors, stop at each one.
My eyes are crossed and squiffed!

I'll give it my best shot I said,
but my results were poor
My lift has broken down and now
I'm trapped on the first floor

We'll see what's happening, she smiled.
Urodynamic test
We fill you up and wire you up
then let you have a rest

I'm filled up with a plastic tube,
then wired to a machine
She told me I should just relax while
numbers fill the screen

Let's see what's what, the young nurse said.
She'd a lovely bedside manner
She's pressing on my bladder now and
swipes me with the scanner

And now there's only one old song that's
hurrying through my brain
It's Engelbert with 'Please release me,
Let me go again!"

The magic toilet now at last, for
measuring the flow
Just sit down there the young nurse said.
Of course I couldn't go

Computer says your bladder's weak.
That isn't news to me
A minor op is what it needs.
A sling to help you wee

10 months to wait to get it done
unless you want to pay
10 months of living on the run,
the Tena Lady way!

I'm not going to vacuum until Dyson make
a sit and ride.

Finally in this section, we're all lucky if we have that special friend, someone who not only knows where the bodies are buried, but will help to bury them. She knows who she is....

Best Friend

Best friends forever, through fat and through thin
More fat, though we tried every diet
We know when to talk or to laugh or to shop
And when to shut up and be quiet

The weddings, the tissues, the men and the hurt
No topic for us is forbidden
We know where we've come from and know
where we've been
And we know where the bodies are hidden

The children we raised, who are now grown away
We cried through those teenager dramas
We've giggled we've danced and we've drunk
loads of wine
And talked through the night, in pyjamas

With hot toast and marmite we shared all our fears
With tea we can put our worlds right
We know from one word on the phone how we are
And will be there half-way through the night

Bits And Pieces

I describe some of these poems as 'challenge' poems.
They are ones that arise from those conversations
occasionally held in the pub, which end with 'I bet
that would make a good poem.'

Beer is living proof that God loves us,
and wants us to be happy

Benjamin Franklin

The first is one such poem, and the pub conversation was whether belly button fluff is always blue. Extensive research on the internet, came up with the following results which I've included in a poem:

Navel Wars

The innies and the outies started fighting
About which shape of navel is the best
The innies said the outies are quite shameless
As their outies make a bulge beneath their vest

The innies on the other hand are neater
Their belly button forms a little dimple
While outies have a great big umbilicus
Sticking in their middle like a pimple

The outies said their version was hygienic
They don't get filled with dust and other stuff
An Oz librarian called Graham Barker
Spent twenty years collecting navel fluff
He saved his in a jar each time he showered
His latest harvest's more than 20 grams
He's got it in the Guinness Book of Records
An easy record, with no real exams

Growing fluff is mainly for the men-folk
It isn't always blue, just try comparing
It's coloured by the towels that you use
And the jumper and the vest that you are wearing

If piercing is your hobby, all shapes do it
Both rings and bars give many people pleasure
Though belly dancers always like an innie
It makes the best container for their treasure

The navel orange has a glorious outie
A recipe for this that will entice
Is fuzzy navel cocktail; mix the orange
With vodka and then peach schnapps over ice

When navel gazing, shape is not important
The organ used in this sport is the brain
But innies say their shape is that much better
Their hollow can be filled up with champagne

So you decide for innies or for outies
But wise advice for both, and please don't scoff
Never unscrew anybody's navel
'Cos if you do their bottom will fall off

*Life is pleasant. Death is peaceful.
It's the transition that's trouble-
some.*

Isaac Asimov

This is another challenge poem, following a conversation with someone whose friend had been widowed.

Before he died her husband suggested she wore some of his ashes in a locket. As the marriage had not been particularly successful for many years the widow did not take up his suggestion. She said she'd had him hanging round her neck for quite long enough!

All of these options are available for ash disposal – at the time of going to print.

Willing the Ashes

An urn up on the mantelpiece is now so out
of date
The Garden of Remembrance could be my
ashes fate

A golden locket for the ash was vetoed by
one wife
She said she'd had him round her neck all of her
married life

For disposal of my ashes I considered
different ways
I could make a Viking longboat then sail
it off ablaze

Or have them sprinkled on a hill or planted
with a tree
Or thrown from a hot air balloon and scattered
out at sea

An artist could mix them with paint, and then
on my behalf
She'd put them in a portrait from a favourite
photograph

Or if I had £10,000 and fancied being bling
Just make a brilliant diamond, cut and mounted
in a ring

Should I will them to a potter who'll glaze them
in a bowl
Or make a garden sculpture with a special
ashes hole

A key ring for my other half to keep in his
back pocket?
No!
Just take me up on Primrose Hill,
explode me
over London
in a rocket!

Sex and golf are the two things you can enjoy even if you're not good at them.

Kevin Costner

This poem speaks for itself....

R 1 P Joey

Oh what is the point of pet budgerigars?
With their bell ringing, squeaking and squawks
They can't frighten burglars or curl on your lap
Or take you for long healthy walks

Oh what is the point of a budgerigar?
Does its little caged life have a meaning
It chats to itself in the mirror a lot
And spends its life flapping and preening

Oh what is the point of a budgerigar?
It's just made of feathers and fluff
It spills all its seeds on the floor of the cage
Plus feathers and yuckety stuff

Oh what is the point of a budgerigar?
It's hard to tell girls from the boys
They flap and they hop, ring the bell all the time
And just make a horrible noise

Oh what is the point of a budgerigar
They are the most pointless of birds
Some proud owners claim to have taught
them to speak
But it's usually just very rude words

Oh, what is the point of a budgerigar
With their feathers and funny shaped
beaks
So just put a blanket on top of the cage
They'll think that it's night time for weeks

The brain is a wonderful organ;
it starts working the moment you
get up in the morning, and does
not stop until you get to the of-
fice.

Robert Frost

The Tea Rooms of England

The ladies who lunch are a disparate bunch
They've looked after families for years
Now hubbies play golf and the children are grown
So they've signed up to be volunteers

The garden and stately home cafes of England
Rely on their catering skills
To pay for your walnut and coffee gateau
There's volunteers staffing the tills

Guided tours for the trust, selling lavender bags,
Jars of honey or tea towels or soap
And joining new members, or giving short talks
Are all in the volunteers' scope

They charge entrance for gardens, run charity
shops
Push ward trolleys, serve meals on wheels
The middle-aged middle-class volunteer crew
Do the lot in their sensible heels

Filling envelopes, walking, or knitting up squares
Are jobs they consider worthwhile
The middle-aged middle-class ladies of England
Do all that they can with a smile

Royal weddings and jubilees, sporting events,
Brought tourists to view by the score
The gift shop and cafe tills pinged without cease
As the money rolled in more and more

The nature reserves and the large stately homes
Had thousands of teas to provide
The middle-aged middle-class ladies of England
Just put on their pinnies and sighed

The middle-aged middle-class ladies of England
Go unnoticed by people who shop
Till they said, hold on now, this just isn't fun
All this working so hard has to stop

The middle-aged middle-class volunteer crew
Decided to show how they feel
They need recognition, and not to be only
Invisible cogs in the wheel

If the sandwich is stale or the cake is too dry
Or the tea is too cold or too strong
It seems that the volunteers always get blamed
Only noticed when something goes wrong

The middle-class middle-aged volunteer gang
Decided that they didn't like
Being blamed for the problems or else being ignored
So the volunteers all went on strike

'We are not invisible', 'What about thanks?'
Were some of the slogans they chanted
The middle-aged middle-class ladies of England
Were tired of being taken for granted

The tea rooms and cafes were empty and dusty
In gift shops the cash tills were silent
The volunteers marched and waved placards
and sang
But they wouldn't do anything violent

The national debt grew as tourism fell
The face of the countryside altered
The gardens grew weeds and the lavender died
The British economy faltered

The prime minister called an emergency state
The queen went on TV and pleaded
'Without you the tourism industry fails
You're specialist skills are so needed'

A new law was passed, for the brave volunteers
A medal for all those who serve
The middle-class middle-aged volunteer crew
Have the thanks that they truly deserve

Old Wives' Tale

An apple a day keeps the doctor away
This adage should come with a warning
I ate 30 last Tuesday to last for a month
And the doctor was round the next morning

The only difference between me and a
madman is that I'm not mad.

Salvador Dali

This poem was written for a competition with this title – it didn't win, but did get published in an anthology!

It's a Colourful Life

My grey matter is tickled pink now we have the green light
to demonstrate this title's truth; prove it in black and white

A blue moon's when it gets the chance, it revs up purple prose
A technicolour chance to chase those brightly hued rainbows

It's got the rose-tint glasses on to paint the town bright red
The grass does not look greener now, just blue-eyed times ahead

It's blue sky thinking from now on; come bolts from out the blue!
A golden opportunity, as shiny thoughts come through

The flying colours shimmer near, like on the silver screen
It's psychedelic Christmas lights, the brightest ever seen

So near and yet so far away, my brain starts
blacking out
Browned off that the ideas won't fix, it's seeing
shades of doubt

Some red wine and some white as well might
help it find its way
Pink elephants float in the air,
as life goes back to grey

Life may have no meaning, or even
worse, it may have a meaning of
which I disapprove.

Ashleigh Brilliant

Happy New Same Ole Same Ole

I've made the same old promises,
I do it every year
I'm going to give up chocolate
and cigarettes, and beer

I've bought a ten-gear mountain bike,
I got it in the sales
And drawing-pinned my weight chart
to the wall behind the scales

I'll do more sport, some jogging and then
join the local gym
And swim at least four times a week,
by next year I'll be slim

The garden needs some working too,
by summer we'll be fine
And early nights from now on,
off to bed by half past nine

Rubbish TV's banned, just
documentaries and news
Buy worthy books, no spending cash
on lipstick, bags and shoes

Paperwork will all get done,
I'll shift that paper stack
And housework every day, I'll dust and
polish, clean and vac

It's healthy food from now on in,
no pizza junk or chips
Only organic healthy stuff will
ever pass my lips

I don't know who I'm kidding, 'cos
last year I recall
By the evening of the thirteenth, I
finally broke them all

This year then, my ambition is
to keep it up for longer
Till January fourteenth just to
prove my will's got stronger

Why is it that when you trans-
port something by car, it's called
a shipment, but when you trans-
port something by ship, it's called
cargo?

Anon

Any Answers?

At the Fawcett Inn pub quiz
on each Tuesday night
The teams are all desperate to win
I've read Wikipedia and learnt loads of stuff
So I hope that my questions are in

I know that:
Three Catherines, two Annes and a Jane
were Henry the Eight's set of wives
A butterfly tastes for its food with its feet
And cats sleep two thirds of their lives

The Wizard team always come first in the quiz
They all have IQs that are high
My team is the Funsters, we try very hard
But never quite seem to get by

I know that:
Hadrian's wall was first built
to keep out the Picts and the Scots
An adult girl cat is a queen or a molly
And pointillists only use dots

The quizmaster's started,
the first round is pop
We try hard but can't quite recall
The name of the oldest of all of the Beatles
John, George or Ringo or Paul

I know that:
Rats are unable to vomit
The first Star Trek film was Man Traps
Sir Isaac worked out how the universe works
And then he invented cat-flaps

The next round is sport, and the quizmaster asks
Hot-dogging is found in which sport?
We giggle and smirk , but our answers don't work
It isn't as rude as we thought

I know that:
Lester Piggot won 9 Epsom Derbies
And starfish don't have any brain
Florence Nightingale did the first ever pie chart
And twenty two yards make a chain

The questions are finished we've not won again
The Wizards are still the top team
It's yet more revision, I know we can win
Or maybe that's only a dream!

This one's a cuckoo in the nest, as it wasn't written by me, but by my Uncle Stanley when he was a student in the 1950s. Thank you for allowing me to include it Stanley.

Cobalt Blues

I am an artist, I live in a garret
And dry bread is most of my diet.
But painting, I find, is no use any more,
If I paint something, no-one will buy it.
I've tried painting landscapes,
I've tried painting nudes,
Pop art, still life and the rest;
Now I'll tell you what happened
to some of these things
And you'll realise why I'm depressed.

I set out one day with a landscape in mind,
I chose a large hill, steep and bare.
With a valley below, and tall mountains above
And the scent of the pines in the air.
I set up my easel and started to paint,
Then the ground gave a sort of a jerk.
An avalanche started, but I didn't run -
I was carried away with my work!

I painted a picture at art school one day,
It was called 'Bacchanalian Revels'.
It typified vice, was disgusting and crude;
It was full of nude women and devils.
When the art teacher looked and she saw what I'd done,
She blushed, and her cheeks were aglow,
She drew a black line right across it and said
'One must draw the line somewhere, you know!'

Modern art! Now at last I had found, so I thought,
My niche in the artistic world.
I squared and I circled in red, blue and green,
And in yellow, I squiggled and squirled.
I held exhibitions in Morecambe and Deal,
Llandudno, St. Ives and in Brixton,
But the only thing I ever managed to sell
Was the palette my colours were mixed on!

I decided to paint a still life so I put
A small plate of fresh fruit on a stand.
With everything ready, I started to paint
With a steady and confident hand.
But you know what it's like when the spirit is weak;
You are hungry, your stomach implores.
My picture, I fear, had an orange peel plus
One banana skin, two apple cores!

So here I am starving, the candle is low,
I am hungry; I haven't a friend.
There's a rope round the rafters, I've made up my mind,
And I've just tied a noose at the end.
I shall stand on a chair, put the noose round my neck,
(It's a pity I've got to die young);
As I jump off the chair, I shall have this last thought:
It's the first time I've ever been hung!

Stanley Dobson

I have never managed to perform this poem; even trying at home is too difficult, perhaps I should only do it after actually drinking half a gallon of home made wine. Strange, but quite a few of my poems seem to feature wine!

Wine Making

Elderflower, blackberry, greengage and plum
We've lots of home made country wine
With just yeast and sugar and water and fruit
Our health drink is coming on fine

It has to be tested, the elderflower first
It's sparkling and golden and clear
We try just a sip, but we can't be quite sure
We've waited for this for a year

We pour out another glass, still looking good
This second glass goes down quite well
We must have a third, though the colour was good
We forgot to test that one for smell

It's smells quite delicious so we have some more
My fourth one goes in a pint glass
My husband seems tired and the next thing I know
He's outside, flat out on the grass

This love is sho winely I'll jusht try shomore
To make sure it really ish ready
I go and join hubby out there on the grash
My legsh both feel stightly unsleady

We start shinging Beatles, their Yeshterday tune
But middle our worms sho it'sh wrong
Our neighbour calls 'stop all of that bloody row!'
But I don't know the words to that shong

Thish tine wasting's fun, but it makes you tite quired
We're both feeling mellow and merry
The elderflower sheems to have all dishappeared
Tomorrow it'sh plum and blackberry

Those are my principles, and if you
don't like them well I have others.

Groucho Marx

This was written as a rather angry response to a writer at a poetry night, who said he was surprised there wasn't any proper poetry, just verse!
Most of the poets there were comic poets, the complainer's poem featured clergy, death and ruminations on the after life…..

Real Poetry?

No graveyards, no clergy, no nightingales trill
I have no lonely clouds and not one daffodil
No wanderings and ponderings of my inner pain
My purpose, dear friends, is to just entertain

I don't pretend, listeners, my feelings are deep
I've no epic poems to send you to sleep
If you crave strong emotion, I fear I have none
For me, lovely audience, poetry is fun

I'm all in favor of keeping dangerous weapons out of the hands of fools. Let's start with typewriters.

Frank Lloyd Wright

I live in Warwickshire, and this poem tells the story of the strange phenomenon of the mop fair, so a bit of a history lesson follows, if you can be bothered to read it.

The Warwick Mop-Fair since 1351

The Black Death reduced populations by half
And wealthy employers just couldn't find staff

Oh the mop-fair, Warwick mop-fair, where they
don't sell mops

Edward the third wrote a labourers' charter
Folk couldn't move house or earn money
by barter

Oh the mop-fair, Warwick mop-fair, where they
don't sell mops

Each year men were told just how much they'd
be paid
So they came to the mop-fair with tools of
their trade

Oh the mop-fair, Warwick mop-fair, where they
don't sell mops

If the job wasn't right and it felt a dead loss
You could come back next week, and then find
a new boss

Oh runaway Warwick mop-fair, where they still
don't sell mops

Now the mop-fair is back in the town twice
a year
With fairground rides, sideshows and hog-
roasts and beer

Oh the mop-fair, Warwick mop-fair, where they
still don't sell mops

The mop-fair is a twice-yearly fair held in the
Market Square in Warwick and various other
midlands towns. In Warwick the first mop is held
on the first Friday following October 12th.
Edward III wrote a labourers' statute in 1351
forbidding workers to move. This was intended
to keep wages low as, following the massive
population losses during the Black Death, labour-
ers were able to command higher and higher
wages. Edward's decree was aimed at helping
the wealthy.
The chancellor would announce the maximum
annual wage every year in the town-square, and
workers would come to be hired carrying a
tool of their trade so employers could recognise
them. Hence a milkmaid might carry her milk-
ing stool, a carpenter a saw and servants carried
mops or brooms. If they were hired they were

given a coin and a badge ribbon. The money was spent on the food and sideshow stalls set up by locals.

If the new job didn't work, for either employer or boss, then the runaway-mop was a week later. If you were hired at this fair then you had to stay with your new employer for the whole year.

In modern times the fair is still held, though now it is purely entertainment. The town is full of mechanical rides and sideshows which appear on Friday night and disappear on Sunday morning – to return a week later for the runaway

Two thirds of Americans can't do fractions. The other half, just don't care.

Anon

Feathery Friends

Twitchers are wild about birdlife
If it's feathered they can't get enough
of each call and song
their lists are quite long,
and they all know their twite from their chough

The ornithological twitcher
can name birds by feathers or flight
the nests or the eggs
or the colour of legs
and they all know their chough from their twite

There are two different kinds of people
in this world: those who finish what
they start, and . .

Brad Ramsey

92

Insomnia

The road to Sleep is a short one
So why
do my feet stumble
and find new paths
to explore and lead me away
from my desired destination?

The best cure for insomnia is to
get a lot of sleep.

W. C. Fields.

Am I alone in thinking?

Am I alone in thinking I'm not worth it?
Is it just me refusing to take care!?
Am I the voice who won't say it with flowers?
A loner who will never go compare?

Is it my solo thought that it's not simples?
I won't try something different today?
The best a man can get is not a promise
I don't need help to work and rest and play

I'll make a drama out of any crisis
I won't join with the ladies that go crunch
Love it or hate it works for every product
And when I take a break it's for my lunch?

Am I the only one who won't just do it!?
And puppies on a roll to me seems mad
It's not the real thing, I'm not just lovin' it
Am I alone in thinking we're being had?

Sometimes the road less travelled is
less travelled for a reason.

Seinfeld

94

Many poetry competitions limit the number of lines you can do. This was an entry for such a competition.

Paved With Good Intentions

I'm going to write a poem and I'll do it in ten lines
I have to study meter, couplets, assonance and rhyme

I need to use poetic words like gossamer and zeal
And make it sound emotional, yet down to earth
and real

Metaphor of toughened steel will sharpen up
my prose
With similes as bright as stars, as gentle as a rose

From rapture to the soulful depths of gloom, or
even worse
The reader will be transported in just a single verse

My words will touch your very soul, you'll find you
shed a tear
Prepare to be amazed my friends, I feel my muse
is near
I'm going to write a poem and I'll do it in ten.....
oops!

Sometimes I Just Sits

After breakfast I decide to sit awhile
I haven't visited my garden since
autumn swept in
A cold, grey January morning welcomes me
To my favourite bench
My breath clouds in the air as I sip
hot sweet coffee
A few raspberries cling to a straggled shoot
And a foolish wallflower blooms in the rockery
My neglected plants gently ask to be tended
But it is not yet time for me to nurture them
In a few weeks they can be shaped and nourished
But now, I sit
No thoughts visit my mind
I feel at peace
When the thought that I am cold slowly
starts to form
I go inside
My house welcomes me back
Still smelling of toast and coffee

A gentleman is a man who can play
the accordion but doesn't.

Anon

This poem has a science lesson included.

I've always been fascinated by woodlice, and when a fellow poet revealed that he believes his animal familiar is a woodlouse, this poem was the result.

Armadillium or the not-so-common woodlouse

Close cousin to the shrimp and prawn but land-
bound, where it's damp
You're all that I could ever want, articulated champ

Each breath I take is just for you, my leg gills feel
vibration
Escort me to the compost heap you sexy, wild
crustacean

Just wave your curved antennae
and drum gently on my shell
Then take me, isopoda, do that thing you do so well

Wrapped in your seven pairs of legs,
I'm closer to my god
Your exoskeleton drives me wild,
terrestrial arthropod

Just curve your platelets over mine,
and wrap me in your legs
I'll follow to the wood-pile
where we'll brood and hatch our eggs

We'll cuddle up all winter long, rolled tightly in a

ball
Cold weather and the hairy spider won't scare
us at all

My Tiggyhog, brave Chuggy-pig, you make my
blue blood hum
Oh Armadillo, Armadillas, armadillium.

Some facts about Armadillium
Genera Woodlice are terrestrial crustaceans. They
are isopods, with 7 pairs of articulated legs and a
segmented exoskeleton.
Mating - The male waves his S shaped antennae to
attract the female, then drums on her exoskeleton
with his front legs before mating.
Ammonia excretion - Woodlice do not produce
urine but excrete ammonia gas through their
exoskeleton to save energy by not converting to
urea or uric acid. Woodlice (apparently) have an
unpleasant taste similar to "strong urine."
Coprophagy - Woodlouse blood is blue as it

contains copper, rather than iron as in mammals. Woodlice eat their faeces. to reabsorb rare copper which bacteria then change to a form absorbed back into their bodies.

Drinking through the anus - Woodlice get water with their food, drinking through their mouth or using their uropods. These are tube-like structures on the posterior of the animal. To drink they press their uropods close together and touch against a moist surface. Capillary action pulls the water up into the anus.

They also absorb water vapour directly through their exoskeleton. In regions of high humidity they can become water logged and then move to less humid areas.

Sense of smell. - Woodlice are able to detect chemical odours using sensory receptors on their antennae

Changing Sex - Male woodlice infected by Wolbachia bacteria will turn into females! The bacteria upset the normal action of the woodlouse male hormone, this process means that there is a better chance of Wolbachia survival as all infected offspring will be female.

The next poem is by another family
member - my talented sister Nett.
Thank you Nett.

To Dementia

Bit by bit
It started with a single word - a word I
tried to use
I couldn't find it anywhere and so I had to
choose
Some other words to use instead - to
make my meaning clear.
I had the word just yesterday. I know that
it was here.

Bit by bit
You stole the time, but left the clock still
standing in its place,
And craftily you left the hands still creep-
ing round its face
And pointing to the numbers . Though I
looked all that I saw
Was a clock which wouldn't tell me what
the time was any more.

Bit by bit
You hid the Latin names of my beloved trees
and shrubs
And the pretty English names of all my plants
in pots and tubs.
And though I sit and stare at them for what
can feel like hours
All you've left me in my garden is some
greenery and flowers.

Bit by bit
You knew how I loved reading so it really
was unkind
To take the stories from my books - but
leave the words behind.
My magazines and newspapers mean nothing
any more
So they gather dust - a pile of useless paper
on the floor.

Bit by bit
And then you took my husband - the best
friend I'd ever had
He was always there to comfort me and
stop me feeling sad.
The man you left looks just the same, but I
don't understand
Why he shouts at me and grabs my arm and
pulls me by the hand.

Bit by bit

I faded from the mirror hanging on the bed-
room wall
'Til the face that looked back out at me -
just wasn't me at all.
It was a sad old woman's face with hollowed
cheeks and eyes.
Though I was shocked to see her there, the
face showed no surprise.

Bit by bit
Life got so confusing - you moved everything
around
And the streets I used to know so well were
unfamiliar ground.
You even moved my house and when I
knocked on my front door
A woman came and said I didn't live there
any more.

Bit by bit

You stopped me going to the shop - the one
place I was known
And now they say I shouldn't try to go out on
my own.
The shopkeeper was kind and took my hand
along the street.
His jacket hid my breasts, but not my shame
nor my bare feet.

Bit by bit
My confidence just disappeared, as did my
sense of pride.
My dignity, my sense of self I'd rather I had
died.
My books, my plants, my poetry - the things I
loved so well.
You've taken everything I had and left an
empty shell.

Annette maxted

Wine Science

The remarkable science of wine
Means that hormones and wine are reactive
And after three glasses or more
All sorts of men look quite attractive

The second rule cancels the first
When we've had a few glasses to drink
Though all men look better to us
Our charms are much less than we think

I never think of the future.
It comes soon enough.

Anon